अज्ञातोपनिषद्

Rhythm of X

Sushrut Badhe
&
Prof. (Dr) Sampadananda Mishra

Published by

Midam Foundation

First Edition: 2025

Published by Midam Foundation,

1st Floor, Midam Ashram, K.P. Natham Pondicherry - 605102 India.

E-mail: midamfoundation@gmail.com

ISBN: 978-81-943838-8-8

Price: 163/-

TABLE OF CONTENTS

तस्माद्वा एतस्मादात्मनः आकाशः सम्भूतः ।

आकाशाद्वायुः ।

वायोरग्निः ।

अग्नेरापः ।

अद्भ्यः पृथिवी ।

पृथिव्या ओषधयः ।

ओषधीभ्योऽन्नम् ।

अन्नात्पुरुषः ।

द्वितीया ब्रह्मानन्दवल्ली, तैत्तिरीयोपनिषद्

"This is the Self, the Spirit, and from the Spirit ether was born; and from the ether, air; and from the air, fire; and from the fire, the waters; and from the waters, earth; and from the earth, herbs and plants; and from the herbs and plants, food; and from food man was born"

—Sri Aurobindo (CWSA 18:226)

ACKNOWLEDGEMENT

To Sri Madhusudan Damleji for the inspiration.

To the esteemed Sanskrit scholars Sri Murali Krishnan and Sri Abhinav Kadambi for supporting the Sanskrit translation of an amateur.

To co-author Dr. Sampadananda Mishraji for refining and rewriting the Sanskrit translation.

To Smt. Rakhee Gupta of Krishna's Delight family for proof reading the English poetry.

To eminent colorectal surgeon, Dr. Ashwin R for the beautiful art.

To Sri Dishen Patel for the most apt deisgn for the epilogue.

To Chitra Badhe for helping with the final proofing of this book.

And last, but not the least; to the unknown who is making life's path slowly known.

FOREWORD

I have been connected to Mr Sushrut Badhe through Dr APJ Abdul Kalam, whom he admired, and being co-author of his autobiography Wings of Fire[1] got attached to me. I have not met him in person, but we have exchanged writings over the years, where ancient literature is our common ground. When he asked me to write this foreword, I found it incredible, and I was writing a letter to him expressing my inability when "something" made me write this instead. The Ajñātopanishad is about that something.

We know little about life and live it superficially, drawn into our little dramas, enjoying our dreams, and lamenting when they fall apart. Sushrut was born to doctoral parents and is an engineer. He has been fortunate to live under a guru, Shri Madhusudan Damle Ji, doing what he loved to do as a livelihood. No wonder he is "allowed" to enter the "rabbit hole" the way Alice did in Lewis Carroll's novel[2], and what he "saw" there, he has written here – "The God question does touch everyone, most folks wonder and question; Is there one?" (Prologue 1-2)

A simple question is asked here, akin to what the child asked when he saw the emperor without clothes, supposedly wearing "a magic apparel specially made for him at great cost" and praised for its magnificence by the people; half of them were fearful and half ignorant. "But its logic understands not the soul's cause nor its source. (2. 18).

The DNA we carry in our body have come from our ancestors, and if we count them from our mother and father's side, we will have over 1000 in the last 400 years. Forget about the number when the Upanishads were written because you cannot handle that. Your birth is the "resultant vector" of the Brownian Motion[3] of many thousand life stories where hardly anything could have been missed. "'X' amasses every individual experience and adds to its phantom database. (2. 47-48)"

So, nothing is unknown, only hidden away by Maya[4], "coded and passed on" to manifest in this and future lives in myriad forms—minerals, animals, and humans. "The macrocosm and the microcosm were both verily gelled; all of existence, this mystic 'X,' verily upheld. (2. 69-70)"

Advances in artificial intelligence, robotics, and materials science will continue to play a crucial role in this evolution. Humanoids will not be robots; they will be Homo Deus[5], gods descended from the mortal world, unaffected by hunger, ageing and disease. "'X' is a common entity compositely found in all matter that exists beyond the skies and underground." (2. 63-64)

Unless one chooses to live blind, the Gandhari[6] way, how can quantum physics be ignored that has exposed the fallacy of the material world and demonstrated the continuous transformation of energy-material and proving the oneness of the creation. At the nano level, "science" can "see" a flower, a stone, and an insect, which are the same. Undoubtedly, at the pico and femto levels, materiality will be seen as the primordial plasma phase. "Other material states, elements originated from a primordial plasma phase. (2. 80)"

Our imagination stopped at the "Big Bang" and how materiality manifested through the universe's expansion – galaxies, stars, their planets, very hot, icy, big and small, and so on. And someday, the expansion will be reversed, and all will be imploded into a Black Hole. We are scared to imagine anything behind the Bing Bang and beyond the Black Hole. "All the dots connect no matter how wide they scatter. (2. 96)"

I guess that in the next few decades, human intelligence will be separated from neurons into silicon, and rather than one mind – be it Newton, Einstein, or Mr Gates, or Mr Musk – collective minds will take the evolution forward here and on other planets where the "fragile human bodies will not be required to carry the intelligence. Mankind had a purpose, as Dinosaurs must have had before becoming extinct. "He was chosen to lead as per the 'Grand Plan.'" (Epilogue 16) as Ajñātopanishad says clearly and concisely.

Most Sanskrit literature, especially ancient ones, is written anonymously and credited to Shri Veda Vyasa. While this was a selfless way of doing great work, it removed the intellectual ownership celebrated and fought for in the modern world. For Sanskrit literature to be created and flourish, authors must own up to their work, stand for scrutiny and gain credibility.

I am happy to see Mr Badhe come out with this writing. Of course, he is guided by Sampadananda Mishra, renowned Sanskrit scholar and the Director of the Centre for Human Sciences at Rishihood University, Haryana. Earlier, Mishra was the director of Sri Aurobindo Foundation for Indian Culture (SAFIC), Puducherry, and must have internalised the spirit of Sri Aurobindo.

There is nothing I have read written so beautifully and so true. I wish and pray many more writings come from this blessed duo.

aruntiwari.com

Prof. Arun Kumar Tiwari is an Indian missile scientist, author, and professor. He has written 30 books and co-authored five with Dr. APJ Abdul Kalam, former President of India, including his celebrated autobiography, Wings of Fire.

---

[1]**Wings of Fire:** Kalam, A.P.J. Abdul, and Arun Tiwari. *Wings of Fire: An Autobiography.* New Delhi: Universities Press, 1999.

[2]**Lewis Carroll's book** *Alice's Adventures in Wonderland* is a beloved children's novel about a young girl named Alice who falls down a rabbit hole into a fantastical world filled with peculiar creatures and whimsical adventures. The story explores themes of curiosity, identity, and the absurdity of life.

Carroll, Lewis. *Alice's Adventures in Wonderland.* London: Macmillan, 1865.

[3]**Brownian motion:** Brownian motion, a fundamental concept in stochastic processes, describes the random movement of particles suspended in a fluid. The resultant vector of *Brownian motion* combines multiple independent Brownian paths, illustrating how these random movements can be represented as a single vector in a multidimensional space. This concept is crucial in various fields, including physics, finance, and mathematics. Karatzas, Ioannis, and Steven E. Shreve. Brownian Motion and *Stochastic Calculus.* New York: Springer, 1991.

[4]**Maya:** The Sanskrit word "maya" traditionally signifies "illusion" or "magic," often referring to the concept that the physical world is an illusion and not the ultimate reality. In philosophical and spiritual contexts, particularly within Hinduism and Buddhism, "maya" denotes the deceptive nature of the material world and the transient aspects of existence. Mishra, B. K. *Understanding Maya: An Exploration of Illusion in Indian Philosophy.* Delhi: Motilal Banarsidass, 2005.

[5]**Homo Deus:** *Homo Deus: A Brief History of Tomorrow* explores the future of humanity, examining how advances in technology and science might redefine what it means to be human. Harari discusses the potential rise of artificial intelligence, biotechnology, and the pursuit of immortality, raising profound ethical questions about the future of civilisation. Harari, Yuval Noah. *Homo Deus: A Brief History of Tomorrow.* London: Harvill Secker, 2015.

भूमिका

जीवनमेकं रहस्यम्। तद्विषये च विचारयितुं केवलं मानवा एव समर्थाः। पुस्तकमिदं मुख्यतया श्रीअरविन्दस्य कैश्चित् संस्कृतसूत्रैः प्रेरितमस्ति, यानि पश्चात् 'श्रीअरविन्दोपनिषद्' इति नामके पुस्तके श्रीअरविन्दाश्रमस्य संस्कृत-कार्यालयेन प्रकाशितानि। 'Rhythm of X' इति नामकं पुस्तकमिदं तस्य एव जिज्ञासोः साधकस्य कृते रचितं, यः सामान्यमानवजीवनस्य अन्तरङ्ग-स्तरे अन्तर्निहितस्य गूढछन्दसः अन्वेषणे रतः। अपि चायं तेषां प्राक्तनानां महाद्रष्टृणां सन्देशस्य सारं प्रदातुं विनम्रः प्रयासः, यं सन्देशं ते पृथिव्याः सर्वजीवानां सामूहिक-अभ्युन्नतये पारस्परिक-प्रगत्या च प्रदातुं प्रायतन्त।

अस्य संस्कृताभिधानम् 'अज्ञात-उपनिषद्' इति वर्तते, यतो ह्येतद् उपनिषदां विषयवस्तु बहुलम् आश्रयते - विशेषतः ईश-केन-माण्डूक्य-कठ-तैत्तिरीयोपनिषदां चिन्तनतः यथा अवबुध्यते। अस्मिन् गुरुशिष्यसंवादोऽपि विद्यते। गुरोश्च सम्बन्धः डॉ. नीरोदबरणेन सह श्रीअरविन्दस्य पत्रव्यवहारात्, गुरु-दामलेवर्यस्य आचरणाच्च अत्यधिकं प्रेरितः। सः सर्वदा सुलभः प्राज्ञः सुहृद् वर्तते। विनम्रतया इदं प्रतिज्ञायते यत् अयं ग्रन्थः पाठकं तस्य अज्ञातस्य 'X'-तत्त्वस्य विषये गभीरं चिन्तयितुं तत्र प्रवेष्टुं च समर्थीकरिष्यति, यस्य उपयुक्तः संस्कृत-पर्यायः 'अज्ञातम्' इति, यच्च अस्मिन् ब्रह्माण्डे नूनं विद्यते।

वेदना तादृशी एव भाषा, यया दौर्भाग्यवशात् वयं सर्वे स्वमानवानुभवे सुपरिचिताः स्मः, अपि च जीवने वेदनायाः महत्तमो हेतुः भवति मृत्युः। पुस्तकमिदं मृत्युसम्बन्धि प्रश्नाहतेन एकेन दुःखार्तेन जिज्ञासुसाधकेन सह आरभते। स्वस्य अन्धकारे, स गुरोः प्रकाशम् अन्विष्यति, यः गुरुः तदा मृत्युसम्बन्धि प्रश्नस्योत्तरं ददाति — जीवनमेव।

INTRODUCTION

Life is a mystery and only we human beings are capable of pondering over it. This book is primarily inspired by a select set of Sanskrit aphorisms of Sri Aurobindo which were later titled 'Sri Aravindopanishad', and was published by the Sanskrit Karyalaya of Sri Aurobindo Ashram. This book 'Rhythm of X' is written for the inquisitive seeker of the mystic rhythm that is embedded beneath the surface of an apparently ordinary human existence and is a humble attempt at sharing the crux of the message that the great seers of the yonder years have strived to share for the collective advancement of all life on earth through mutual progression.

Its Sanskrit title is "Ajñātopaniṣad / अज्ञातोपनिषद्" as it borrows heavily on the theme of the Upanishads; as understood from reflections upon the Isha, Kena, Mandukya, Katha and Taittiriya Upanishads. There is a guru shishya dialogue as well and the relation of the guru is inspired from Sri Aurobindo's correspondences with Dr. Nirodabaran and also heavily from guru Damleji's demeanour; he is forever a wise friend who is ever accessible. It is modestly claimed that this book should enable the reader to dwell and delve into the concept of the unknown 'X' whose apt Sanskrit equant is 'Ajñātam' which very much exists in this universe.

Pain is a language that all of us are unfortunately, too aware of in our human experience, and the biggest source of pain in life is death. This book begins with an inquisitive seeker in pain, touched by the question of death. In his darkness, he seeks the light of a guru who then parts the answer to the death question- Life itself!

प्रस्तावना

ईश्वरविषये प्रश्नः सर्वेषां मनसि उत्पद्यते। अधिकांशजनाः आश्चर्यवत् प्रश्नं कुर्वन्ति “किं वास्तवतया ईश्वरः अस्ति” इति। जनानां जीवनम् ईश्वरोपलब्धिना अथवा तद्विना व्यतीतं भवति।

परन्तु उत्तरं सर्वदा मूले एव निहितं वर्तते। प्रियजनस्य हानिः सर्वदा जीवनं प्रति अस्माकं दृष्टिं परिवर्तयति।

यदा च कोऽपि प्रियजनः स्वजीवनात् बहिर्गच्छति, तदा दुःखग्रस्तः व्यक्तिः आध्यात्मिकजागरणस्य अनुभवं करोति। प्रियजनप्रस्थानमिदम् अस्मान् जीवनस्य सामान्यसुखददिनचर्यायाः बहिः क्षिपति।

पुनः प्रियजनं द्रष्टुम् असमर्थाः वयम् आहताः दुःखिताः च भवामः। दुःखे वयं स्वजीवनस्य मार्गम् अन्वेषयामः। प्रियजनानां स्मरणीयक्षणान् स्मरामः। परन्तु ते अतीव दूरे दृश्यन्ते। वयं स्वाभाविकतया सुखदक्षणान् अन्वेषयामः, दुःखस्य औषधं च अन्वेष्टुं संघर्षं कुर्मः।

वयं प्रश्नं कुर्मः "यदि अस्माकं प्रेम शाश्वतम् अस्ति तर्हि सत्यं किमर्थं पूर्णतया न ज्ञायते?" अस्य प्रश्नस्य कारणात् हृदयं स्पन्दते। अतीतस्मृतिषु आसक्ताः भूत्वा वयं वर्तमानं नाशयामः।

यदा प्रश्नस्य समाधानं कदापि न भवति तदा बहवः दैनन्दिनजीवनस्य कार्येषु व्यापृताः प्रश्नस्य उपेक्षां कृत्वा नूतनान् अनुभवान् अन्वेषयन्ति।

परन्तु प्रश्नस्य अग्निः अल्पानां सरलहृदयानां जनानां कृते प्रज्वलितः एव तिष्ठति। एतेन जनाः सस्मितं जीवनम् अभिवादयितुं प्रयतन्ते। यदा यदा प्रियजनानाम् अभावः स्मर्यते तदा तदा ते संघर्षं कुर्वन्ति। ते शीतान्धकारे उष्णप्रकाशं अन्विष्य भ्रमन्ति। यात्रायां ते प्रथमं दुःखं स्वीकुर्वन्ति। ततः ते परिपक्वाः भूत्वा स्वचेतनाम् उत्थापयन्ति।

बहुकालं रोदनेन तेषां नेत्राणि शुष्कानि भवन्ति।

भावावेगान् अतिक्रम्य आशावन्तः ते आकाशं पश्यन्ति।

ते शुद्धतमे उदारतमे सर्वोत्तमे च प्रेम्णि निमग्नाः अज्ञातस्य पवित्रान्वेषणे रताः भवन्ति।

PROLOGUE

The God question does touch everyone,
Most folks wonder and question; Is there really one?
They bide time, in a life with or without meaning,
But the answer lies, always in the beginning.

Life's meaning is always, by a grave loss, shaken,
A dear departed, many times makes the spirit awaken
Suddenly, the event pushes us off our comfort zone
No more do we see, ones who were once, our own.

Hurt and broken, we try to find the way
Longing and pining for memories that seem far away
We then naturally seek moments that never come again
Helplessly seeking a medicine for emptiness and pain.

"If our love was and will always be true,
Why doesn't the truth appear in our full view?"
The heart palpitates when these questions are unanswered
And reminiscences the past, leaving the present shattered.

While these questions more often remain unresolved
For many, in the flux of busy lives, they are dissolved
They choose to ignore and seek experiences anew
But the questions remain burning, for a sincere few.

ASHWIN~

They grapple and try to smile, greeting their daily life
But the presence of absence brings forth a perennial strife
In search of warmth and light, wandering in cold darkness
They mature and transcend, embracing sadness! |24|

They stop wiping their tears, once their eyes turn dry,
With the emotional fog cleared, they then turn to the sky
Holding onto their love, the finest, purest and best
In the search of the unknown begins their sacred quest! |28|

प्रथमो भागः

अज्ञातोपनिषद्

अन्धकारे साधकस्य प्रश्नाः आगताः –

केचन युवावस्थायां गच्छन्ति केचन च वृद्धावस्थायाम् ।

परन्तु सत्यमिदं चिरन्तनम् । दुःखमग्नप्रियजनानां त्यागेन स्वदेहत्यागेन च किं वा लभ्यते? कुतः आयाताः ते? कुत्र च प्रयास्यन्ति? किं वा पुनः भवति? न ज्ञायते सत्यमिदम्।

किं गुहान्ते प्रकाशो वर्तते? किं जीवन्नपि मृत्योरालिङ्गनं कर्तुं शक्यते?

हे सत्यप्रकाश! दर्शय मे तद्दिव्यानन्दमार्गम् । अभिलषामि प्रकाशमेव । सत्यमेव च प्रणमामि।

PART 1

In darkness, came the seeker's questions

"Some go young, some go old,
This truth all have to verily uphold
Leaving behind their loved ones in pain,
Casting away their bodies, what do they gain?
From where did they come?
To where do they go? |6|

Also, what do they become?
Answers to these, no one does know!
At the end of the tunnel, is there light?
When alive, can one receive death's insight?
O light of Truth, the path of felicity, please show
I seek the light, to Truth only I verily bow. |12|"

- ASHWIN -

द्वितीयो भागः

ज्योतिषः समायाति गुरोरुत्तरम्

“प्रहिलेकेयं सदाऽसमाहिता आधुनिकविज्ञानेन। यतोहि न स्वीक्रियते एतेन विकासशीलस्य आत्मनः समुपस्थितिम्। मनुष्ये आत्मनः अस्तित्वं विकासं च अवगन्तुम् असमर्थत्वात् ।

परलोकगतं सर्वम् एतस्य कृते अदृष्टमेव। पिपीलिकायां गजे च प्राणशक्तिं तु पश्यत्येव, किन्तु आत्मनः हेतुत्वं वा मूलं वा एतस्य तर्कातीतम्।

ईश्वरे अविश्वस्तानां स्पष्टोक्तिरियं यत् अनर्थकानि एतेषां प्रश्नानाम् उत्तराणि। नानामतावलम्बिनः जन्ममृत्योः सिद्धान्तप्रतिपादकाः केचन जीवनं नाम शापं शाश्वतपीडा च इति वदन्ति। अन्ये च मृत्युरेव मोक्षः इति। अन्ये केचन स्वपापपुण्यानुगुणम् आत्मा स्वर्गं वा नरकं वा प्रति केनापि नौचालकेन वाह्यते इति विश्वसन्ति। अन्ये च आत्मनः आध्यात्मिकं सत्यं परिभाषन्ते। केचन आत्मनः परलोकगमने साधकत्वं बाधकत्वं च किमिति निर्दिशन्ति।

कथं वा ज्ञातुं शक्यते, किं सत्यम् इति?

को वा मार्गः अनुसर्तव्यः, को न इति निश्चेतुं दुष्करम् । सामान्योऽहं नरः, न दिव्यः पुरुषः, न गुरुः, न अध्यात्मप्रणेता, न वा कश्चित् निश्चितमार्गप्रवर्तकः।

अहं यत् पश्यामि तत् वदामि न तु यद् विश्वसिमि — परन्तु मम समीपे व्याख्यानार्थं विस्तृताः सारांशाः न सन्ति । अतः मम वक्तव्यं शृणुत— तदनन्तरं यथेष्टं स्वमार्गं निश्चिनुत ।

यत् स्पन्दमानं हृदयं मयि वर्तते तत् ममेति वदामि। तथैव अस्ति सर्वपशुषु शुनके वा शूकरे वा। मम फुफ्फुसाः प्राणशक्तिसञ्चारे तथैव सहायकाः यथा जलस्य अधः मत्स्याः श्वसनपराः। प्रत्येकं तृणलता-वृक्षादिषु सा एव प्राणशक्तिः प्रवहमाना।

प्रत्येकं जीवेषु प्रवहति सा समा प्राणशक्तिः। तस्मात् जीवति सर्वम्। सा अस्ति मयि, त्वयि, सर्वेष्वपि जीवेषु। किं द्रष्टुं शक्यते त्वया मद्वत्?

तदेव अज्ञातं अद्भुतं सर्वत्र विद्यमानं, सर्वभूतेष्वपि क्षुद्रेषु महत्सु वा। यतो हि तदज्ञातं सर्वत्र विद्यमानं, तन्नास्ति अनभिज्ञं घटनाक्रमस्य ।

सर्वव्यापि अज्ञातमिदं सञ्चिनोति सर्वविधां व्यक्तिगतानुभूतिं वर्धयति च स्वकोषं स्वानुगुणम् ।

अतः एतत् 'अज्ञातम्' सर्वज्ञत्वेन सर्वद्रष्टृत्वेन च उपास्यते। एतत् सर्वेषु सामान्यं कारकं भवति। परन्तु वयं जानीमः, एकमेवैतदज्ञातमद्वितीयम्। अज्ञातं 'तदेकम्' इति प्राचीनशास्त्रेषु वर्णितम्। आदिस्पन्दात् हिरण्यगर्भात् जगतः उत्पत्तिः इति शास्त्राणि वर्णयन्ति । अस्मात् च पञ्च तत्त्वानि उत्पन्नानि ।

प्रथमं आकाशः उदभूत् । आकाशे गतिप्रभवात् वायुः जातः । वायुघर्षणेन अग्निः जातः । यद् उष्णम् आसीत्, तत् कालान्तरेण शैत्यवशात् जलं जातम्। जलं वनस्पतिजन्तुमनुष्याणां जीवनस्रोतः अभवत् । एवम् 'अज्ञातं' तत् सर्वतत्त्वानां पृथ्वीस्थसर्वभूतानाम् मूलम् अस्ति। चराचरं जगदिदं तस्मादेव उत्पन्नम्।

'अज्ञातम्' इति प्रकृतौ सामग्रिकं सामान्यसत्त्वम्। अधोलोकादूर्ध्वलोकपर्यन्तं सर्वेषु च द्रव्येषु वर्तते अज्ञातमिदम्।

पुरा मुनिभिः परमम् इति प्रोक्तम्। अनुभवलब्धं ज्ञानमिदं बहोः प्राचीनकालात् वर्तमानम् अस्ति । अनेन सिद्धान्तेन जगत् आश्चर्यजनकस्वप्नवत् भासते।

तस्य च सत्यं स्थूलसूक्ष्मलोकानां कृते महत्वपूर्णम् आसीत्। सूक्ष्मं स्थूलं च संयोज्य 'अज्ञातम्' इदं प्रत्येकस्य अस्तित्वं धारयति।

किन्तु आधुनिकविज्ञानं सर्वेषु जीवेषु जडेषु च एकमेव कारकं जानाति। सः चराचरेषु तत् प्रत्येकञ्च प्रारूपम् एकत्र धारयति। आदौ तत् लघुतमम् अविभाज्यपरमाणुतत्त्वम् इति आधुनिकविज्ञानेन घोषितम् आसीत्। अनन्तरं तत् परमाणुतत्त्वम् अनेकैः उपपरमाणुभिः संरचितम् इति अधुनिकविज्ञानेनावगतम्। पुनश्च एतानि उपपरमाणुतत्त्वानि मौलिकतत्त्वसंवलितानि। परस्परसंयुक्तानि नियतरूपाणि च।

एतेषां मौलिकतत्त्वानामासीत् कश्चित् विशिष्टारम्भः। केनचिद् बृहद्विस्फोटनेन एव विश्वसृष्टिः इति विज्ञानेन उद्घोषितम्।

तद्विस्फोटनादनन्तरम् अन्तरिक्षे गत्यारम्भः जातः येन विस्तारः समभवत् । सर्वाण्यपि भौतिकद्रव्याणि तत्त्वानि च मौलिकादुष्णसत्त्वाज्जातानि । सर्वादौ निर्मितपरमाणोः नाम विज्ञानेन 'हाइड्रोजन्' इति स्थापितम् । कालान्तरेण अनेकानि गुरुतरतत्त्वानि सम्भूतानि । येषु 'ऑक्सीजन्' नामकं किञ्चित् घनीभूतम् अणुतत्त्वं समुत्पन्नम्। अतिशयतापवशात् ज्वलनशील 'हाइड्रोजन्' अणुद्वयस्य ज्वलनशील' ऑक्सीजन्'तत्त्वस्य एकेन अणुना सह रहस्यमयसम्मेलनेन जलसृष्टिः समभवत्। एवम् अग्नेः जलस्य रासायनिकं, भौतिकं, रहस्यमयं च जन्म । तदेव जलतत्त्वं पृथिव्यां सकलप्राणिनां जीवनकारणम् अभवत्। यत्र यत्र जलं तत्र तत्र वनस्पतयः पशवः च उद्भूताः। आधुनिकवैज्ञानिकैः प्रतिपादितः सूर्यसदृशः हिरण्यगर्भः पुरातनतारकाणां अवशेषः इति मन्यते। ब्रम्हाण्डस्य एषा बौधिकी संकल्पना यादृच्छिकघटना एव न तु परिहासात्मिका। सर्वत्र ब्रह्माण्डे विद्यमानानि रहस्यमयानि मौलिकतत्त्वानि दिव्यचित्राकृतिरिव

स्वप्नकल्पितानि इव वा भान्ति। ब्रह्माण्डस्थानि सर्वाण्यपि दृश्यादृश्यद्रव्याणि परस्पराद् दूरस्थान्यपि सूत्रे मणिगणा इव परस्परसम्बद्धानि।

यद् रहस्यमयं कणम् आधुनिकविज्ञानं स्वहठधर्मानुगुणं विश्वसिति, यस्य अस्तित्वं च सर्वेषु जडेषु वर्तते, अपरं च यद् अज्ञातम् अस्माभिः दृष्टं, ते उभे समाने अभिन्ने च। अतः तस्य कणस्य 'अज्ञातम्' इति नामकरणं यद् अस्माभिः कृतं, तत्राहं कमपि दोषं न पश्यामि।

एवं सर्वगतं तद् अज्ञातं न केवलं जीवानां ज्ञाता, जडस्यापि आधारभूतं तत्। किं सर्वज्ञः सर्वव्यापी किमपि कर्तुमसमर्थः भवितुम् अर्हति ?

नूनं न । यः सर्वज्ञः सर्वद्रष्टा सर्वानुभवी सः सर्वं कर्तुमकर्तुं च समर्थः।

तदज्ञातं सर्वभूतस्थम्। मनुष्याणां शुभाशुभेषु सुखदुःखानुभवेषु सततं विद्यमानम्। सकलकर्माकर्मनियामकं तदज्ञातं, यद्यपि मनुष्याणामन्तः बहिश्च सततं विद्यमानम्, तथापि उद्भ्रान्ताः मनुष्याः तदनभिज्ञाः। स्वमायया भ्रान्तिं जनयत् तदज्ञातं सुखदुःखानुभवद्वारा मनुष्यान् अज्ञावस्थायाम् असचेतनावस्थायां च स्थापयति। स्वपरमावस्थायामटलं तदज्ञातं मनुष्याणामन्तःस्थम् अपि दूरस्थमेव भाति। सर्वं सामरस्ये स्थापयितुं सर्वथा समर्थं तदटलम् अज्ञातं स्वैकान्तवासम् उपभुङ्क्ते। एवं सर्वं कर्तमकर्तुं च समर्थं तदज्ञातं सचेतनतया मनुष्याणां कर्माकर्मव्यापारेषु आत्मानं न नियोजयति।

एवं च मनुष्यः स्वभारं स्वयमेव वहेद् इति भ्रान्तिं जनयति।

सर्वसमर्थः सर्वज्ञः सर्वव्यापी च निगूढं वसति यतो हि सः गूढव्यापारव्यापृतः। न तु स्वाभिलाषायाः पूर्त्यर्थम्, अपितु मानवजातिं यन्त्रवत् उपयुज्य सचेतनतया सम्प्रेरयन् च स्वभव्ययोजनायाः सिद्ध्यर्थमेव। उचितानुचितमनुभवसमूहं संचित्य उदासीनवदासीनः सुखदुःखादीन् अनुभवति । अज्ञातं तत् शुद्धचैतन्यं तद्वद्विभजति, यथा त्रिकोणीयकाचः श्वेतप्रकाशं विविधवर्णेषु विकिरति।

यद्यपि व्यावहारिकदृष्ट्या सर्वेऽपि न समानाः, तथापि एकस्माच्चैतन्यादेव वयं सर्वे समुत्पन्नाः। अज्ञातस्यावगमनं मानवीयतर्कातीतं विचारातीतं च। तत् तु मनसः परं गत्वैव सम्प्राप्यते। परन्त्वज्ञातम् एकमेव निश्चयेन परिभाषयितुं वर्णयितुं च शक्यते।

PART 2

And from light came the Guru's answer

"This is a puzzle science can never resolve,
For it accepts not that the soul exists to evolve.
Beyond the material physical it cannot see
It's blind to the soul's omniscience in all things that be,
As it recognizes in ant and elephant, life's movement and force
But its logic understands not the soul's cause nor its source.

The atheists bluntly state the answers are not of any worth
But many religions postulate theories of death and birth
Some claim life to be a curse, an eternal damnation[1]
While others state that only in death lies the real salvation
Some speak of the boatman[2] ferrying souls to heaven & hell
Others have metaphysical realities of the soul to state and tell.

Some speak of the fields of transit[3] that block and aid the way
And of the solstices and the solar and the lunar pathway
But of these what is true, how can one know?
One wonders whose philosophy to follow, to whom do we go?
A simple man I am, not a divine teacher
Neither a gnostic leader and definitely not a preacher.

I state what I see and not what I believe,
But I have no elaborate summaries to weave
So, listen to what I have to say
And then you are free, to choose your own way.
Within me is a beating heart, that I can call mine;
So too, it is there in all animals, from the dog to the swine! |36|

My lungs too breathe air, like the gills do for those in the sea;
Just like the life force flows in any weed, creeper or tree,
In every life that lives, there is a sameness that persist,
By virtue of which all life on earth exists.
It is in you, I and in every creature living
Can you see, this common factor that I am seeing! |42|

This same mystic thing say 'X' is present in all
And this ‘X’ is Omnipresent in every life — big or small.
Now, when the same 'X' is present everywhere,
It cannot be unaware of what happens when and where.
Pervading all this, ‘X’ amasses every individual experience;
And adds to its phantom database, as per its convenience. |48|

Thus, this phenomenon 'X' is not just omnipresent,
Because of its all-pervading nature, it is also omniscient—
Thus, this 'X' is both all-knowing and also all seeing.
The common factor of life in all the beings living,
But we know of an unknown that is second to none,
And ancient scriptures describe the unknown as ‘The one’! |54|

A womb-golden[4] that stirred universal expansion from a primordial sound
From which *Prarkriti's*[5]/nature's five elements[6] were verily found!
The *Vayu*/winds began to expand from its unknown *Akasha*/space
And from the airy friction, the birth of *Agni* took place
Fire cooled slowly and from its condensation arose *Jala*/water
And *Jala* gave birth to life on earth; in plants and animal matter. |60|

Thus, unknown is the source of all the elements and all life on earth
From it, the living and non-living have taken birth.
So in *Prakriti*, 'X' is a common entity compositely found
In all matter that exists from beyond the skies to the underground,
It was declared to be supreme, by the wise ancient sages
And this knowledge of the unknown, was known over the ages. |66|

Its conceptual brilliance made the world appear like a dream[7],
For its truth embellished both the subtle and gross physical realm,
The macrocosm and the microcosm were both gelled,
All of existence, this mystic 'X' verily upheld. |70|

But science knows a factor in all the living and non-living
Holding together the structure in every animate & inanimate being
It was first declared 'Atom'— the foundation of life indivisible
But later on discovered to be infinitely divisible. |74|

Made up of elementary particles held together
Having a fixed pattern and relation with one another
But these fundamental particles had a unique beginning
Science preached of a big loud explosion that created everything

And in space, the expansion and movement began taking place
Other material states, elements originated from a primordial plasma phase. |80|

Initially there was only gaseous Hydrogen[8]; highly inflammable
Which over time, birthed heavier elements including Oxygen — another molecule combustible
At great temperatures, two Hydrogen molecules combined with one Oxygen molecule mysteriously,
From fire, water was born physically, chemically and mystically.
And this liquid became the source of all life on earth
Where water was, plants and animals took birth. |86|

The principle of uniformity[9] that the modern cosmologists view
Does appear useful in bridging the ancient and new
The truth declared by scientists of the modern ages
Somehow corresponds with that of the ancient sages.
The golden womb is eerily similar to the old star relics — like the sun
Surely this intelligent design wasn't made by fluke or for fun. |92|

As if a matter of a divine art or a surreal fantasy
Mystic fundamental particles are present in every galaxy
Across the cosmos in every light and dark matter[10]
All the dots connect no matter how wide they scatter. |96|

This 'mystic' particle that science is religiously believing
Whose pattern is present in all things living or non-living
And the 'X' that we saw are one and the same

So I see no fault in giving it too, the 'X' name
Thus, the omnipresent 'X' is not just the knower of the living,
It is also the foundation stone of existence of the non-living. |102|

But can the omniscient-omnipresent be incapable of something?
Nay, the all-knower, seer, all experiencer can do & undo everything!
So, this 'X' is present in all things, that are good and also bad
In all the life experiences, irrespective of whether happy or sad!
Reigning unknown to man, in all his life's order and confusion
Within him and yet of it, he remains in ignorant illusion. |106|

Keeping man confused and deluded
In joy and sorrow, 'X' keeps man unaware and excluded
Maintaining a status quo in its supra-mortal existence
It dwells inside man and is yet at a distance.
Despite being capable of putting to order any confusion,
Unmoved, it dwells seemingly in an aloof seclusion. |112|

Thus, the all-capable 'X' consciously chooses to not interfere
Creating an illusion that life's burden, man has to alone bear |114|
The all-capable — omnipresent-omniscient dwells covertly
Only because it is up to something secretly
Not to fulfil its own whim, like an instrument it uses man,
Consciously driving him to fulfil its grand plan
Amassing a mass of experiences wrong and right
Experiencing both pain and joy, with its detached insight. |120|

Like a prismatic refraction of a great beam white
Into the creation 'X' splits consciousness in every shade of light
Though, morphologically and practically all aren't the same
From the same consciousness all of us came
To understand X is beyond man's logic or thought
Only by going beyond the mind, can the realization of X be got! |126|

But this definition of X can be certainly made
And of 'X' it can be verily declared and said. |128|

---

[1]**Eternal damnation:** Many modern religions and cults speak of life on earth as a sin and a curse of God and that the true experience of a heaven is possible in another world only.

[2]**The boatman:** In Greek mythology, *Charon* was the boatman who ferried the souls of the dead across the River Styx or the *River Acheron* to Hades

[3]**The fields of transit:** Certain spiritual texts have talked about the kinetics of the post life journey and the various planes of consciousness and how the journey is affected or aided by an individual's karma and/or other factors. For instance, the eighth chapter of *Bhagavad Gita* speaks in detail about the post life journey of Yogis and how the solstices (northern/ *Uttarayana* or the southern/ *Dakshinayana*) aid or impair the journey of yogis determining whether they get liberation/mukti or re-birth.

[4]**Golden—womb:** It is a reference to the Upanishadic & Vedic term of 'Hiranyagarbha'; the brilliant primal golden womb that manifested the entire creation

[5]**Prakriti:** She is the Divine Feminine is the eternal counterpart of The One who is The Divine Masculine. All living ones, irrespective of their gender identifications are considered to be one and a part of the divine feminine as per the Bhagavad Gita and other Sanatana Dharmic/ spiritual texts.

[6]**The five elements:** This is a reference to the Vedantic 'Pancha Maha Bhootas' and the sequence of formation of the elements (Ether/Akasha, Wind/Vayu, Fire/Agni, Water/ Jala, Earth/Prithvi) is as it is, from the Taittriya Upanishad which was written several thousand years ago. The original Sanskrit verse has been printed on the first page of the book along with a translation by Maharshi Sri Aurobindo.

[7]**Maya:** A reference to Maya; the divine illusion which prevents a human's realization of God on earth

[8]**Hydrogen:** The first chemical element in the modern Periodic table maintained by the IUPAC (International Union of Pure and Applied Chemistry). According to Astronomers, Hydrogen was the first element that was formed moments after the big bang. Hydrogen comes from the Greek words hydro meaning "water" and genes meaning "forming". Hydrogen, a diatomic molecule, is the principal constituent in an intriguing chemical reaction, which chemical engineers call a combination reaction where 2 molecules of hydrogen combine with a molecule of oxygen to give a molecule of water; the molecule of life.

[9] **The principle of uniformity:** Also called the doctrine of uniformity, it is a metaphysical postulate that defines a spatiotemporal uniformity in the natural laws and process that occur across the cosmos. It is very difficult to verify by scientific methods.

[10]**Dark matter:** It is a mysterious existence theorized by astronomers and physicists which is considered to be entirely invisible, emitting no light or energy, making it undetectable by conventional sensors and detectors. It is believed by many scientists who study the properties of dark matter that it is composed of black holes as it does not react with baryonic matter except through the force of gravitation, better known as gurutvakarshanam.

- ASHWIN -

तृतीयो भागः

निष्कर्षः

अज्ञातमेव सर्वभूतस्था प्राणशक्तिः तस्याः कारणं मूलं च। शरीरे प्राणशक्तेः प्रवेशः तस्याश्च पुनः बहिर्गमनं तस्य अज्ञातस्य कारणादेव सम्भवति। तदेव पुनः कारणं सम्भूतेः विनाशस्य च। तदेव समन्वयात्मकमज्ञातं सर्वमप्येकसूत्रेण बध्नाति, तदेव सृष्टौ निहितं चैतन्यम्। तदेव सर्वव्यापकं सर्वज्ञं सर्वदृक् च सर्वस्य स्रष्टृत्वेन प्रवर्तकत्वेन च तिष्ठति। मायाजालात् मुक्त्यर्थम् अज्ञातस्य ज्ञानं तदर्थं जिज्ञासा च अपेक्ष्येते। विज्ञानेन यत् नाविष्कृतं तस्यान्वेषणं, अज्ञातस्य रहस्योद्घाटनं चात्र ध्येयं येन जगदिदं उपदेष्टुं शक्यते।

एतेन प्रकृत्या सह सङ्गतिं विधाय स्वजीवनं नियतं कर्तुं शक्नोति, येन मानवजातिः विकासयात्रायां चरमावस्थां प्राप्तुं शक्नोति। विजिगुप्सां विभाजनं च विनाशयितुं, ऐक्यभावेन प्रगतिं कर्तुं समृद्धिं च प्राप्तुं, सामरस्यम् ऐक्यं च अनुभवितुं, सामूहिकस्तरेषु दिव्यचेतनां प्रतिष्ठापयितुं च अयं प्रयासः। अज्ञातस्य तस्य ज्ञानार्थम् आवश्यकता मया प्रतिपादिता । निष्ठापरतया मया मम बोधः दृष्टिकोणश्च प्रतिपादितौ । किम् एतत् भवतां कृते उपयोगि न वा कृपया स्वकीयं विचारं प्रकटयन्तु।

PART 3

Conclusion

X thus seems to be the life force
And also its cause and the source
Coming in and going out of every living body
The cause of birth and death for everybody
Holding matter together, it is the cohesiveness
In the creation, It is the inherent consciousness. |134|

All pervading, all knowing and all seeing —
Creator and perpetrator of everything
'X's' understanding will have to be gained and sought
To escape from the illusion in which man is caught,
To find the answer that science never got
To unveil the spirit's secrets so the world may be taught. |140|

So, man can learn to regulate his life in sync with nature,
For humanity to evolve man to its highest stature!
To erase the lines of hatred and division
To ensure man can prosper and progress in unison
To experience the spirit of harmony and oneness
To collectively manifest in all, a divine consciousness. |146|

The need to realize 'X', I have shared to you
Sincerely I have shared my understanding and view
Did you find it useful in any way?
Were any of your questions answered, do say?" |150|

ASHWIN

चतुर्थो भागः

समुपलब्धिः

शिष्यः प्राञ्जलिः संसन्तोषम् उदघोषयत्—

तदज्ञातं परमं श्रेष्ठतमं दिव्यं च इति मया समुपलब्धम्। अतः तदज्ञातमेव दिव्यम् इति वक्तुं न शङ्के। अस्माकं जीवनस्य सर्वेऽप्यनुभवाः परमादेव समुत्पद्यन्ते तस्मिंश्च लीयन्ते। मृत्युरेव जीवनस्य बहुमानं करोति। अत एव जीवनस्य क्षणं प्रतिक्षणं मधुमयं भवति। मृत्युरेव कर्मचक्रप्रसारकः, न तु अस्माकं जीवनयात्रायाः अन्तिमं पदचिन्हं पूर्णविरामो वा। जानाम्यहम् एकदा ममापि जीवने परिवर्तनस्य तदेव क्षणमागच्छेदिति। अतः तावताहं यथार्थं निष्कपटं च जीवनं जीवेयम्। इदानीम् एतदेव जीवनस्य मे चिरं ध्येयम्।

अद्य द्विजोऽहं, नवचेतनायां मे जन्म, जीवनस्य नवारम्भः, नवोषःकालः च । मामकाः येऽपि इतः प्रतिगताः सन्ति, जीवनेऽस्मिन् न तेषां पुनरागमनं इति ध्रुवम्। परन्तु ये चात्र जीवन्ति तेषु नैके वृथा दुःखिताः। न मदर्थम् अपि तु जगद्धिताय स्वदुःखं त्यजेयम्। इदानीं दिवा वा निशायां वा, जीवने एकमेव ध्येयम्—सकलदुःखनिवारणम्। जीवनस्य प्रतिक्षणं भवेत् कार्तज्ञ्यभरितमहोत्सवः। अपि च जीवनस्य प्रत्येकं कर्म भवेत् नवोत्साहभरितं भगवते अर्पितं च।

दिव्यचेतनायाः पूर्णोपलब्धये काङ्क्षेऽहं भवितुं सूर्यसमः शाश्वतप्रकाशधारकः आनन्दभरितश्च। आनन्दमेव प्रसारयितुं जीवेयम् अहं दिनानुदिनम्। एष एव दिव्यमार्गः, दिव्येच्छाप्येषा दिव्यस्य चेयं अनन्तयात्रा।

PART 4

The Realization

The *student* exclaimed in satisfaction, with folded hands:
"I understand 'X' to be the ultimate of existences, O So fine
And So I see no hesitation in simply calling it 'The Divine!
From 'The Divine' all our life's experiences originate
And into 'The Divine' all of them culminate.
Death makes life all the more valuable
Making every moment of life most invaluable. |156|

It is but a revolution of the karmic wheel
And not the journey's final destination or seal
I know that my life too will one day end
So until that day, I shall live and not just pretend
This is now, my life's purpose and true meaning
And today is my second birthday, a new dawn and beginning. |162|

The ones who left me, have departed to never come again
But there are so many, who are crying out in pain
If not for my sake, for the world, I can throw my sorrow away,
To alleviate suffering; is my mission every night and day!
Life's every second, I will celebrate in gratitude,
And consecrate my every action with an energy renewed! |168|

To recognize and experience for real, The divine consciousness,
I aspire to become a perineal beacon and sun of happiness!

Only to spread **Ananda**[11]— the bliss of Life, I shall live every day
For I realize this is the Divine's path, will and way". |172|

---

[11]**Ananda:** A steady state of felicity and uninterrupted bliss that is beyond the cycle of joy and sorrow. The Vedas consider Ananda to be a part of the Divine trinity of Sat-Chit-Ananda or Truth- Consciousness and bliss and is the highest destination of every individual born on earth. Maharshi Sri Aurobindo described all living beings as children of Ananda or children of bliss, entrusted with a divine mission of spreading Ananda in life, thus transforming an ordinary life into a superconscious life divine.

A unity of the functions of primes embodying "the golden ratio" itself, the abstraction the three eyed being unfolding nature to showcase reality shaping into evolution fr the point of genesis.

उपसंहारः

अन्ते शिष्यः लिखति प्रारम्भिकम्

परमसत्तायाः निगूढनिश्चलानन्दात् समुद्भूतः प्रणवात्मकः स्पन्दः। स च स्पन्दः आसीत् पुनः निराकारस्य आधारसम्भूतः। तस्मादनन्तादन्तरीक्षं जातं कालोऽपि। तस्मादेव नादात्मकस्पन्दात् प्रकाशान्धकारौ समुत्पन्नौ । दिव्यप्रकाशं ध्वनयितुं जडात् जातानि नक्षत्राणि। कस्यचित् बृहतः शुभ्रनक्षत्रस्य विस्फोटनात् समुत्पद्यते हिरण्मयः सूर्यः।

तस्माच्च विस्फोटनात् नैकेऽपि क्षुद्रग्रहाः अजायन्त, गतिमन्तश्चाभवन्। चन्द्रः ग्रहान् परितः ग्रहाश्च सूर्यं परितः भ्रमितुं आरब्धवन्तः। क्षितिः, आपः, तेजः, वायुः, आकाशः चेति पञ्चमहाभूतानि घनीभूतानि अभवन्। एतेन जीवनाभिव्यक्तेः अवसरः सम्भूतः। एकैकं जीवनम् अनेकत्वे विभजनात् महाप्रपञ्चोऽयम् विकसितः।

अस्मिन्महाप्रपञ्चे एकेयम् पृथिवी यत्र शब्दादेव जीवसृष्टिः समभवत्। वनस्पतयः अविर्भूताः, पशुजगदपि प्रकटितम्। एवं नैकानि राज्यानि विकसितानि, एवं नूतनानाम् आविर्भावः पुरातनानां च तिरोभावः। इयमेव विकासप्रक्रिया प्रचलन्त्यस्ति।

सर्वेष्वपि जीवेषु एक एव मनुष्यः, यः स्वचेतनायां विकासस्य अनन्तसम्भावनायाः कारणादस्यां विकासयात्रायां देवेशितः पुरोहितः। भगवत्प्रसादेन मनुष्यः श्रेष्ठबुद्ध्या मनसा च युक्तः आसीत्। एतेन स्वकर्मणा स्वभविष्यनिर्माणाय भाग्यनिर्माणाय च सः स्वतन्त्रः आसीत्।

स्वतन्त्रताकारणात् सः स्वीयसुखादिकं चित्वा स्वमनसा बुद्ध्या च प्रकृतेः उपरि आधिपत्यं प्राप्तुं प्रायतत। परन्तु कालक्रमेण स्वाज्ञतावशात् नानाविरोधिभावानां विभजनानां च कारणभूतः अभवत्। सः स्वात्मनि सौन्दर्यम्-असौन्दर्यं दैवमासुरं च समकालं परिपोषयितुं प्रायतत।

कालेन स्थितेः प्रतिकूलतावशात् सर्वत्र वैषम्यविस्तारः जातः, विविधोपद्रवाः अपि समुद्भूताः। एतासां समस्यानां परिहारार्थं मानवप्रज्ञा आसीदसमर्था। अस्यां स्थितौ चेतनायाः विकासमतिरिच्य नान्यगतिः। मनसः विविधस्तरं भित्त्वा तदूर्ध्वगमनेन चेतनायाः विकासः सम्भवः इति उपलब्धवान् सः। विकसितचेतनायामेव सर्वाः समस्याः विलीयन्ते।

तदा स्वीयहृदयस्पन्दनेषु श्रुतवान् सः तमेवादिस्पन्दं यस्य कारणात् सृष्टिरियं सम्भूता। तमेव शब्दमाश्रित्य सः चेतनायाः सर्वोच्चशिखरं प्राप्तुं शक्यते। अतिमानसप्रकाशोद्भासितं शिखरं प्रतिगमनमेव तस्याग्रिमं लक्ष्यम्।

EPILOGUE

In the end, the disciple writes the beginning:

From within the inertial stillness of ethereal bliss
The primordial vibrations escaped bodiless lips.
From infinity — space and time were then found —
Darkness and Light were both born of the first sound. |4|

Matter formed stars to echo the celestial light —
A golden sun exploded from a great star — white.
Many tiny planets were set whirring into motion.
Moons around the planets & planets revolved around the sun. |8|

The elements condensed — Earth, fire, wind, water and sky
An atmosphere was created for the manifestation of life
Hastily life forms divided for complex organisms to be found.
One planet witnessed the origin of life from sound. |12|

Ecosystems, habitats and kingdoms – plant and animal appeared
Newer species gradually evolved as older ones disappeared.
Most evolved of them was the species of Man
He was chosen to lead as per the 'Grand Plan.' |16|

Man was blessed with mind and superior intellect
By his actions his future he could shape and select

Man chose Happiness and sorrow, Joy and misery.
With his gifts, even over nature sought he victory.

Next man created unconsciously conflict and divide:
Ugliness and Beauty began to co-exist and reside.
But over centuries, this equilibrium was breached,
Inequality flared as chaos's threshold had reached.

These problems man's wisdom could no longer solve
For in the present state man had to but evolve.
Recognizing the need to go beyond the mind
Evolution was the only panacea he would find.

And then he heard in the beat of his heart
The same sound that brought about the start.
Through it, could he reach the greatest height
The next level he would ascend — the man of supramental light!

ORIGINS

Midam

On 24th November 1996, Sri Madhusudan Damle received the word Midam deep in his meditation. He has described this reception as a literal vision of a descent of three letters "मि द म्". He grabbed a white chit and immediately penned them down with a red marker that was near him, lest he forgets the letters and thus Midam was first materialized. He even made a toran of the words Midam on a paper on the auspicious *'Bhoomi Pujan day'* and put it on the fence.

In 1999, he built his building with the name Midam etched on it and he meditated upon it for hours. Not wanting to himself attribute any meaning to it, over the next couple of years, he approached multiple Sanskrit scholars asking them to share the meaning of this word. Many commented that on shruti, Midam appeared like a maha-mantra of "I am that" but were not able to perfectly state. Some more years passed and Damleji held this mantra close to his heart, keeping it a secret.

One fine day, during intense meditation, he spontaneously called upon the divine asking the divine only to clarify the meaning and immediately he heard the voice- "Don't you know? It is short for "Miraravindashranam mama".

A dashakashra mantra where the first, fifth and tenth letters were respectively "मि द म्". Damleji was satisfied but still kept this a secret from the rest of the world. In 2011, During an auspicious moment of inspiration, Damleji gave Midam a symbol and significance and under his direction, his NGO began the journey for engaging in loka sangraha which birthed several projects like Krishna's Butter Project, Vedic Chants Intervention, Rhythm of Krishna, Learning through nature etc. All these projects though were positively impacting tens of thousands of people across the world, only a handful of individuals had joined the mission and all activities were freely undertaken without even taking donations.

In September 2024, inspired by the work of some senior citizens connected to the Sri Aurobindo ashram who were cleaning up the trash and litter that was being indiscriminately dumped on the beach, Damleji himself engaged in the beach cleaning to join the movement and consciously supported it and on 18th October 2024, he re-organized his NGO founding "The Midam Foundation" to smoothen mass participation and also governmental collaboration for manifesting collective change so all members and volunteers can work "united yet freely" in the spirit of Damleji's modus operandi of free union.

When Damleji first came to Pondicherry in 1988, he heard from many directly or indirectly that this mission of his was just a dream. Not paying heed to detractors, he only smiled and said *"They call it only a dream. Let us all join hands to make it a living truth"*

This become his motto and the dream is being born. He is never in a hurry of things, but when it comes to manifesting a divine will, he works God speed.

ॐ मिदम् ॐ

MIDAM FOUNDATION – OBJECTS

1. Revival of Education systems with Gurukul projects & working with like-minded individuals, NGOs, governmental and private institutions.

2. Creating & aiding projects and conducting research and receiving support for revival of Indian knowledge systems (IKS) in India using latest technologies like Artificial intelligence (AI) and also entering into research collaborations with governmental and non-governmental organizations NGOs, national and international educational institutions and organizations.

3. Research & development of personality development education modules for children and adults.

4. Supporting and advancing projects for Women empowerment and promotion of good health in children by supporting projects for helping underprivileged women, widows and children.

5. Creating and developing a place that can give a serene atmosphere for the advancement of religion, spirituality or yoga.

6. Providing Relief for poor, education, yoga, medical relief and conduct of free medical camps and also donations to individuals and other charitable organizations.

7. Aiding and creating projects for the preservation of environment projects, cleaning drives in cities and rural areas individually or in collaboration with various governmental departments and purchasing of machineries for cleaning of public places and construction of toilets, installations of bins and the likes after obtaining requisite governmental regulatory approvals.

8. Preservation of monuments & articles, places of historical importance.

9. Public awareness projects for promotion of individual well-being in society thorough medical and spiritual camps, blood donation drives, suicide prevention programs etc.

10. Providing education and education material and support in the form of grants and/or donations of books to deserving individuals and people irrespective of caste, creed, or religion.

11. Advancements of projects of public utility and conduct of awareness drives and de-addiction camps for public and working towards elimination of addiction to narcotics, addiction to alcoholic substances.

12. Furthering the projects that advance the research or treatment of animals, development of sustainable practices and innovative methods for promoting agriculture, promotion of ayurveda and ayurvedic therapies in collaboration with organizations, individuals and government departments such as the department of drugs control, AYUSH etc.

13. Supporting shelter homes for the destitute and elderly, supporting special schools, homes and individuals working for the betterment of life for children with special needs, conduct of awareness and sensitization camps for parents of children with special needs and also general public.

14. Rehabilitation support to individuals, families or organizations during natural calamities or man-made tragedies.

If any of these resonate with you, please consider this as an invitation to unite and work together freely.

The aim of Midam symbolized

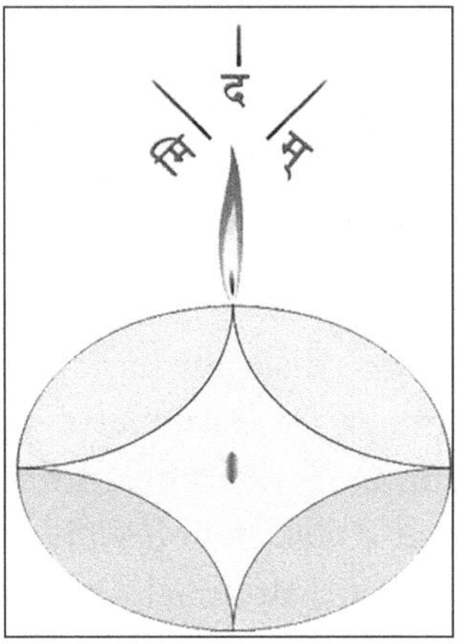

The sphere represents the earth that we live on.

The blue colour (upper hemisphere) depicts the skies and green (lower hemi-sphere) the flora and fauna.

The central yellow arched diamond represents man who is always in communion with the five elements.

Inside man is a tiny flame - the flame of aspiration which represents the Chaitya Purusha – *"the psychic being"*.

Man's aspiration takes him higher and higher to meet the Supreme light represented by *Agni*- the flame.

This higher knowledge descends in man and he then embraces the earth having received this light- the knowledge, and he uses it for the betterment of all life on earth.

About the Authors

Sampadananda Mishra

Dr.Sampadananda Mishra

(https://en.wikipedia.org/wiki/Sampadananda_Mishra) is the Director of Centre for Human Sciences, Rishihood University. He is passionate about Sanskrit and Indian Knowledge Systems. Dr. Mishra has spoken at various conferences, seminars, and literary & religious festivals, both nationally and internationally on Sanskrit, Indian culture, Yoga, spirituality and Education. In addition, Dr. Mishra, as a devotee of Sri Aurobindo and The Mother, is familiar with their writings and feels comfortable in delivering lecture on Philosophy and practice of Sri Aurobindo's Yoga. He has been to USA and other countries several times for giving lectures, conducting workshops and participating in conferences and seminars.

Dr. Mishra worked as the Associate Editor of the Collected Works of Vasishtha Kavyakantha Ganapati Muni published in twelve volumes. Dr. Mishra has founded and launched the first ever 24 hours Sanskrit Radio called Divyavani Sanskrit Radio and is single handedly managing the entire content since its inception in 2013. In the year 2014 Dr. Mishra founded Samskrita Balasahitya Parishad with the aim of creating, evaluating and propagating children's literature in Sanskrit. Recently Dr. Mishra has launched a monthly E-magazine for children in Sanskrit called Saptavarna.

The Govt. of India has conferred the President's award (Maharshi Badarayna Vyasa Samman 2011) on Dr. Mishra for his outstanding contribution to Sanskrit.

In the year 2014 the Ministry of Culture, Govt. Of India conferred the Senior Fellowship Award to Dr. Mishra for carrying out his research on the Vedic Art of Multiple Concentration.

In the year 2017 Junior Chamber International (JCI) India, (JCI Pondicherry Metro) conferred the Literary Excellence Award on Dr. Mishra for his contribution to Sanskrit language and literature.

Dr. Mishra was conferred the Kendra Sahitya Akademi Bala Puraskar for 2018 for his book Shanaih Shanaih – A book of Rhyming songs in Sanskrit for children.

Dr. Mishra was conferred the Pandit Deen Dayal Upadhyaya Recognition of Re-engineering India 2020 by the Re-think India Organisation.

Sushrut Badhe

Sushrut Badhe (https://en.wikipedia.org/wiki/Sushrut_Badhe) is a mechanical engineer who primarily engages in the manufacturing of Ayurvedic products at his master's unit, KVM Research Labs (www.ayurvedaforyou.in). He engages in research related to Sanskrit scriptures and Indian Knowledge Systems (IKS) and has published papers in multiple reputed scientific journals like International Journal of Religion and Health, Molecular Cytogenetics, Natural Language Processing journals, IEEE Access, etc., and he has no idea why he does this.

He also has a good/bad habit of writing poetry in rhymes and likes using the name "Rhythm" in the titles of the books which he writes and releases for free. His books include Rhythm of the Spirit, Rhythm of Krishna, Rhythm of Ananda: Sri Aurobindo's Vedanta, and Rhythm of Veda: Know your Devas. Most of his books are available online at reasonable rates, but if you wish to procure a free PDF of any of his books, you can always send him a good old-fashioned email requesting a copy.

He believes his writing journey started ever since he got to meet his Guru, Sri Madhusudan Damle, during the ending months of 2010, and after he began residing with his Guru, the rhythm of poetry only grew. He also picks up trash (old alcohol bottles, wasted diapers, shoes, plastic spoons and more) as part of the " ❤Clean Earth, Together We Can!" group of conscious citizens who are taking the lead in cleaning up Pondicherry's rock beach.

Some words of request to the readers:

1. Please find your Guru in life (if you haven't found yours yet). This meeting can be a life-changing moment.

2. Please learn how to cook; it's very useful and necessary in life.

3. Have fun and enjoy with friends and family in the company of nature, if you wish, but please don't litter. I would love to have the superpower of picking up all of it with my own hands, but I am far too limited alone.

❤ Clean Earth, Together We Can.